LIGHTNING BOLT BOOKS™

White Everywhere

Kristin Sterling

Lerner Publications Company
Minneapolis

To my friends, with love

Lerner Publications Company
A division of Lerner Publishing Group, Inc.
241 First Avenue North
Minneapolis, MN 55401 U.S.A.

Website address: www.lernerbooks.com

Library of Congress Cataloging-in-Publication Data

Sterling, Kristin.
    White everywhere / by Kristin Sterling.
        p.   cm. — (Lightning bolt books™—Colors everywhere)
    Includes index.
    ISBN 978-0-7613-4592-3 (lib. bdg. : alk. paper)
    1. White—Juvenile literature. 2. Colors—Juvenile literature. I. Title.
QC495.5.S748 2010
535.6—dc22   2009017952

Manufactured in the United States of America
1 — BP — 12/15/09

Contents

The Color White

Do you like clean, simple colors? Many people like the color white.

This mother and daughter are wrapped in a fuzzy white blanket.

You can find white eggs on a farm. Baby chicks hatch from them.

White clouds float through the bright blue sky.

What shapes do you see?

Cauliflower is a
white vegetable.
You can eat it
for dinner.

You can grow white flowers
in a garden.
These flowers are
called lilies.

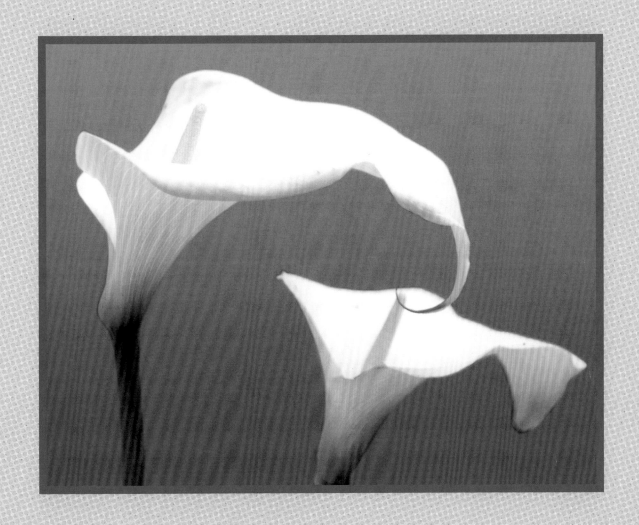

White doves are released at some weddings.
They are symbols of love, faith, and peace.

You can play in newly fallen snow. It covers the ground like a white blanket.

Fluffy white snow makes a soft cushion for playing outside or skiing.

People
also make
things
that are
white. You
can doodle
on white
paper.

Teachers write on white dry-erase boards in classrooms.

Does your classroom or school have dry-erase boards?

A Passion for Paint

Do you like to paint? Artists use white paint to make many colors. You can try it too!

Blend white paint with other colors. You will make lighter shades of those colors.

15

A dollop of white in purple paint will create a soft lilac color. White mixed with blue makes sky blue.

White combined
with red makes the color
pink. A smidge of white in
orange paint makes a lovely
shade of peach.

Experiment with
adding a little white
or a lot of white.
What happens?
It's fun to find out.

The Meaning of White

How do you feel about the color white?

Many important public buildings are white. The White House in Washington, D.C., is the home of the U.S. president.

White can make you feel that everything is clean and in order. Doctors and dentists wear white coats partly for this reason.

This doctor is about to give her patient a shot.

Brides often wear white dresses when they get married. The color stands for hope and innocence.

21

Many girls wear white when they celebrate their First Communion.

Some people feel that white is a holy color. Angels wear white in many religious paintings.

Whitney Loves White

Whitney loves the
color white.

She has a white guinea pig named Snowy.

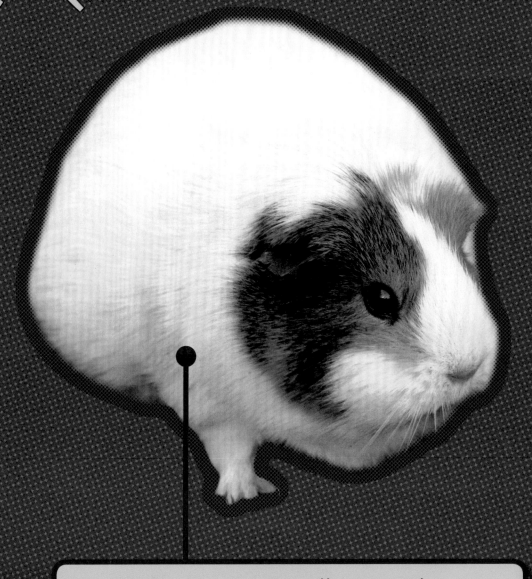

A guinea pig may be all one color or several colors. Its fur may be white, black, brown, tan, or cream.

She has a white computer, white furniture, and white clothes.

She feels rested and relaxed in her white bed.

What is your favorite color?

How We See Color

- Light comes from the sun. Sunlight contains all the colors of a rainbow.

- Light can be reflected or absorbed. When it is reflected, it bounces off. When it is absorbed, it soaks in.

- Some things reflect all colors of light into your eyes. These things look white.

- An apple looks red because it reflects red light into your eyes. All of the other colors are absorbed.

- Oranges absorb every color except orange. Bananas absorb every color except yellow.

- Your eyes see only the colors that are reflected off an object.

Color Blindness

People do not always see colors in the same way. Some people can't see all the colors in the rainbow. Reds and greens look the same to them. These people are color blind. Color blindness is more common in men than in women. Color blindness can be checked with a simple test.

A person without color blindness can see the number in this circle. Look closely. Do you see a 5?

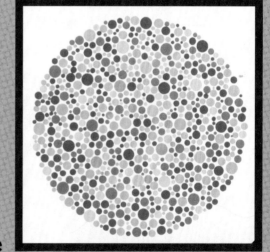

A person who is color blind would not be able to see it. The number would appear the same color as other dots in the circle.

Glossary

dollop: a little bit

doodle: to make a little drawing

experiment: to try something out in different ways

innocence: the state of being pure and harmless

release: to set free

religious: part of an organized faith

shade: the darkness of a color

symbol: something that stands for something else

Further Reading

Brown, Margaret Wise. *The Color Kittens*. New York: Random House, 2009.

Color Roundup
http://pbskids.org/dragonflytv/superdoit/color_round_up.html

Macaulay, David. *Black and White*. Boston: Houghton Mifflin, 1990.

Sterling, Kristin. *Black Everywhere*. Minneapolis: Lerner Publications Company, 2010.

White: Enchanted Learning
http://www.enchantedlearning.com/colors/white.shtml

Index

Photo Acknowledgments

The images in this book are used with the permission of: © Dale Wilson/
Photographer's Choice RF/Getty Images, p. 1; © Hans Neleman/Stone/Getty Images,
p. 2; © Marcy Maloy/Digital Vision/Getty Images, p. 4; © N.a. Planken/Dreamstime.
com, p. 5; © Christian Draghici/Dreamstime.com, p. 6; © Spike Mafford/Stone/Getty
Images, p. 7; © Marta Johnson, pp. 8, 18; © Marlene Ford/Dreamstime.com, p. 9;
© Peter Treanor/Alamy, p. 10; © John Kelly/Digital Vision/Getty Images, p. 11; © ZOOM
(187) Education-Arts/Imagemore/Getty Images, p. 12; © Yellow Dog Productions/Digital
Vision/Getty Images, p. 13; © Hill Creek Pictures/SuperStock, p. 14; © iStockphoto.com/
Chris Rose, p. 15; © Ian O'Leary/Dorling Kindersley/Getty Images, p. 16; © Elisabeth
Coelfen Stills/Alamy, p. 17; © iStockphoto.com/James Group Studios, p. 19; © Monkey
Business Images/Dreamstime.com, p. 20; © Ron Chapple Studios/Dreamstime.com,
p. 21; © Digital Vision/Getty Images, p. 22; © Stockbyte/Getty Images, pp. 23, 25;
© Susan Pettitt/Dreamstime.com, p. 24; © Robert Nolan/Dreamstime.com, p. 26;
© michelleannb/Shutterstock Images, p. 27; © Anatoliy Samara/Dreamstime.com,
p. 28; © Dorling Kindersley/Getty Images, p. 29; © Kevin RL Hanson/DK Stock/Getty
Images, p. 30.

Cover: © Christopher Ewing/Dreamstime.com (dove); © Alistair Scott/Dreamstime.com
(rabbit); © Petros Tsonis/Dreamstime.com (flower); © William Trethaway/Dreamstime.
com (milk); © Péter Gudella/Dreamstime.com (T-shirt); © Todd Strand/Independent
Picture Service (paint strips).